The loud clacking sound of a little girl's dress shoes on wooden stairs, giddy laughter, and a smile that lit up the room. All this wrapped up in the cutest little package with pigtails you've ever seen—with the oldest soul of any eight-year-old you've ever met! It was in this moment that I understood, this was no ordinary little girl. To hear her speak was to hear the voice of someone much more mature than what her age alone would indicate. It wasn't the vocabulary or her superior mastery of grammar for someone so young, but rather, it was the weight of verbal expression that made a statement and left you with an undoubtable knowledge that this little girl spoke with authority coming from experience.

This is not my first memory or interaction with LaNiah, as I have known her all her life. I serve as an associate pastor at the church she and her family attend. I have had the opportunity and privilege of watching LaNiah grow up and even managed to help influence that growth, just a little bit.

LaNiah's life experience and compassionate approach to helping others comes through in her writing and all that she does. This book will compel you, the reader—to open yourself up to the deep-seated emotions and beliefs that keep you from achieving spiritual peace and tranquility. Her raw truth and self-examination will free you to examine yourself with no fear of judgment or condemnation. Each section is filled with truthful examination and followed up with supporting truth from the Word of God. LaNiah has achieved the balance of true introspection with presentation of healing words and principles that can only be derived from God's Word.

LaNiah has been recognized as a leader among high-school-aged students in her community. She has been asked to speak several times at various forums discussing topics such as racial equality and is seen as a peer counselor by many who know her and by the youth in her church. LaNiah possesses not only a maturity that is immediately evident to all who meet her but also a heart of love and compassion that comes through in every conversation and interaction. People are drawn to her and feel welcomed and at ease in her presence. This comes through in her writing as well. You truly feel as though you know her personally when reading her words. She has recently been accepted as a student to Fresno Pacific University and her talent as a writer is going to flourish as a result.

LaNiah has helped to mentor and mature many of the young ladies within the church. Through serving as an usher, performing, ministering on the dance team, and helping with the younger children on Sunday mornings, she is leaving her mark on the lives of many. I have personally listened and watched as she counsels and ministers to others in her peer group. It solidifies all that she shares in this book. She presents a balanced, mature, simple, and no-nonsense way of coming face to face with one's self and applying truths to begin the healing and maturation process. LaNiah is careful not to present herself as a clinician but rather as one providing truth and a pathway to begin the process of loving one's self and others again.

Pastor Tony Noriega
Associate Pastor – Restoration Ministry of Visalia

I have known LaNiah all of her life. When she was a little girl, she was so cute, very talkative, smarter than most children her age, and full of life. Then around third grade something happened to the bright and sunny LaNiah I knew. But I did not know until I read this book exactly what LaNiah had endured.

LaNiah was still beautiful, still smart, but part of her seemed lost—that's how this book started. *The Breaking Point* is LaNiah's journal entries. I told you she was smart.

From the worst experience for any child to the resulting depression and anxiety, LaNiah uses her journals and the Word of God as her journey toward recovery.

Here and now, LaNiah is all smiles. That beautiful, intelligent, fearless, and confident girl is back; only now, LaNiah is a bright young woman ready to take on the world! LaNiah is a leader at her church and in her community, and even without this book she has helped so many young women like her.

But do not be misled. This is not a flowery, "I love God and everything is awesome" type of book. LaNiah is open and honest and confesses some of her present struggles. In the chapter "Love," LaNiah explains how, even now, she tries to avoid physical contact. However, she says every day she is getting better at being affectionate.

In the chapter on anxiety, LaNiah also openly expresses that for her, anxiety and depression were a package deal. They plagued her until she "chose daily to put my faith in God, and with faith in Him, I have nothing to be anxious about."

In the end, LaNiah embraces what every young woman, and human being wants—true happiness.

Growing up in America can be so stressful for young people. The pressure to fit in and the pressure to be perfect is embedded in our culture. *The Breaking Point* shows you how it is possible to overcome this struggle.

I advise you to read this book—read a chapter of each day as a devotional. It will inspire you, it will encourage you, and it will help you overcome.

Camille Slack

During the most challenging times of your life, when you need hope and direction, LaNiah Goodman shines a bright light on the dark hole that can swallow you up and guides you toward the path of joy and restoration. You are about to go on a transformational journey. *The Breaking Point* was written to give you a different view of your world. It is filled with emotions and real-life stories. You will see your reflection in some of her stories, but she will hold your hand through the entire journey. You will be inspired and motivated.

Buckle up as she takes you on a raw, uncut journey into the heart and soul of a teenager's life, as she looks for love, acceptance, happiness, wholeness, and discovers a deeper intimacy with God and the true meaning of "The Joy of the Lord is Your Strength" (Neh. 8:10).

Despite periods of unspeakable and tragic struggles, LaNiah has blossomed into a well-adjusted young lady, full of life, adventure, hope, and a bright future. Her desire is to share what she has learned through her manual so that you won't have to reach your breaking point.

The Breaking Point is an impactful, dynamic, and life-changing book, filled with fresh revelation that will help you overcome your most challenging obstacles. I applaud LaNiah's courage, passion, and commitment to changing lives, and so will you. You will complete this journey knowing that you are not alone, that you will survive, and that you deserve a great life.

Enjoy the Journey!

Lucille Willis
Author of
21 Days of Praise:
Seeking God's Face Instead of His Hand

THE BREAKING POINT

THE BREAKING POINT

LANIAH ROSALIND GOODMAN

XULON PRESS

Xulon Press
2301 Lucien Way #415
Maitland, FL 32751
407.339.4217
www.xulonpress.com

ISBN-13: 978-1-6628-1504-1
Hardcover ISBN-13: 978-1-6628-1505-8
Ebook ISBN-13: 978-1-6628-1506-5

Dedication

I WOULD LIKE TO FIRST DEDICATE THIS BOOK TO GOD. IT IS A JOY TO KNOW that someone loves me so much that He would send His Son, Jesus Christ, to die for me. Regardless of the mistakes I have made, He always forgives me and never holds anything against me. I dedicate this book to Him because He gave the book to me; everything in this book has been something God has either spoken to me or helped me to remember.

I also want to dedicate this book to young Christians. Being a teenager and Christian comes with its difficulties. You get looked at differently because you don't do everything that kids your age are doing. It gets challenging sometimes, but God will always be there to give you strength. It is better to live a life with Christ than without Him, trust me.

I dedicate this book to lost souls. I pray that my story will lead people to give their lives to Christ. When people hear my story, the only thing I want them to hear is how God moved in me and turned my life completely around. I always hear people say that they have done so much bad that God can't forgive them, but honestly, God forgets it all and throws it in the sea of forgetfulness. God gives you a second chance and will change your life; all you have to do is give your life to Him.

Table of Contents

Acknowledgement

THANK THE LORD FOR GIVING ME THIS BOOK. I NEVER THOUGHT I WOULD be writing a book. I was really self-conscious about the book because of how young I am; I didn't think people would take me seriously.

I would like to thank my mother. Without her, I wouldn't know the importance of having a relationship with God, or any of the many other life lessons she has taught me. She has always been there for me and always made sure that I put God first.

I would also like to say thank you to all my aunts and uncles, and my spiritual family at Restoration Ministry, Visalia. Thank you for taking me in as one of your own. They have always shown me an endless amount of love and poured into me a lot spiritually.

To my Auntie Lena and Uncle Jamaine, words cannot express how grateful I am to have you in my life, as well as my cousins Daralise, Katé, Davian, and Laurise. It truly took a village to raise me and I am glad it was you guys.

To my Bishop Robert Hooks/Grandpa, thank you for being not only my spiritual leader, but my grandpa. I am grateful that God put you in my life. Words can't express the impact you have on my life, and I love you so much.

To my siblings, biological or not, I am so glad that I had you all in my life while growing up. Although at times it was difficult, God showed me through you how to love people. I pray that our relationship will grow in the future. You guys are truly a blessing.

To my godparents, I thank you for everything you guys have done for me—for praying for me even when I didn't ask you, guiding me in the right direction, encouraging me, and supporting me in everything I do.

Each person plays a vital role in my life and in some way has helped me to be the person I am today. Words can't express the love I have for them nor how much they mean to me.

Introduction

ON THE DAY OF OCTOBER 16, 2019, I DECIDED TO TAKE MY LIFE MORE SERIously. By "taking life seriously," I mean thinking about the future, especially spiritually; my relationship with God has to become number one in my life. God must always come first.

I have been put in this place where I feel as if I have reached my breaking point. But not just any normal breaking point—I feel that I really can't move forward without change.

In this book, or journal, or whatever you want to call it, you're going to get the absolute, raw truth. No holding back, no sugar-coating. Some of it might be confusing, but bear with me. This book isn't just to spill my guts out. This book is designed to actually help people like me get through some of the hard times—to let them know that they're not the only people that experience these things and have these emotions.

I have actually gotten numerous prophetic words about this book and how impactful it could be to other teenagers my age. It took a lot for me to actually finish it. I started writing this in the beginning of 2019 and finished in the middle of 2020. But I believe there is a reason for this. Maybe it's to keep me going or to help somebody else keep going. Maybe it just might help someone get to know Jesus. This book is my testimony, my experience in my walk with Jesus, and many more things that could possibly help whoever is going to end up reading this. I'm not sure what the plan is after this book, but whatever happens, I know it's going to work out in God's plan.

During the tough times in life, it is very difficult to find hope and figure out what to do.

Trials and tribulation often change our focus. Most of the time we find ourselves trying to solve our own problems and not surrendering them to God.

In this book, I write about numerous emotions that tried to take over me, which I was able to overcome by the grace of God. I was only able to overcome with God's help, of course, but I also drew from the knowledge that was poured into me by my family. There are a lot of people out there who don't have the privilege of knowing the things that I do, so if I can at least help one person, I will do it!

Jesus calls us to be disciples and spread the Word. My goal is to win souls. Having a relationship with Jesus is the number-one most life-changing thing you will ever go through. I aim to give people hope that there is someone who loves them and truly wants to set them free.

> "You then, my child, be strengthened by the grace that is in Christ Jesus, and what you have heard from me in the presence of many witnesses entrust to faithful men, who will be able to teach others also." (2 Timothy 2:1-2)

Loneliness

IMAGINE BEING ON AN ISLAND IN A TINY LIFEBOAT, WITH NO ONE AROUND you; you're sinking and no one's there to save you. That is the closest I can get to describing the way I have felt my whole life. I surrounded myself with people to disguise the fact that I had nobody.

People never understood me. I knew I was different, and no one could relate to me.

Every time I tried to describe to people why I felt lonely, they would brush me off. Since then, I have always kept to myself. No one ever knows what is going on with LaNiah—where I am, what I am doing, how I am feeling. I have learned to be okay with it.

Not everyone is going to be there for you like you think they should. After long years of disappointment and prayer, I am now able to be content by myself.

The crazy thing is that even when I felt like I was alone, I never truly have been. God was always there for me, even when I felt like He wasn't there.

> "Have I not commanded you? Be strong and courageous. Do not be frightened, and do not

be dismayed, for the Lord your God is with you wherever you go." (Joshua 1:9)

Friendships

I USE TO THINK FRIENDSHIPS WERE ONE OF THE MOST IRRITATING RELATIONships any teenager could experience. The real definition of a friend is someone with whom you share a bond and mutual affection; someone you can confide in and who can do the same with you. I feel as though God wants you to have friends. He doesn't want you to feel like you're alone all the time (even though you're not, because God is always present). As believers, we should be friends with everyone, even if they don't accept us as their friends.

Since I was so insecure about not having friends, I always called people my "best friends" without truly knowing the meaning behind it or what it took to be a best friend. I always felt sad when my so-called friends never texted me, checked on me, or asked how I was doing. I never had a friend do that for me; I was always the one to check on them, and that hurt. I never understood how I could be so nice to people and still get walked all over. In Ecclesiastes 4:9-12, it says, "Two are better than one, because they have a good reward for their toil. For if they fall, one will lift up his fellow. But woe to him who is alone when he falls and has not another to lift him up! Again, if two lies together, they keep warm, but how can one keep warm alone? And though a man might prevail against one who is alone, two will withstand him—a threefold cord is not quickly broken."

I always thought that God was trying to teach me a lesson or isolate me so He could get me by myself. Then I went through this phase where I felt like I was too much of a real friend for people to deserve me, which was not a good thing. I had to really ask God to change my heart and give me the right attitude.

I shed so many tears for people who wouldn't even think twice about me. This made me realize that not everyone was going to be my friend. One thing my mom always tells me is once that one good friend comes into my life, I should cherish them because they are very rare to find. God eventually dealt with my heart and told me how I am called to love people unconditionally, friend or not. Even when they do me wrong, I still have to love them, just like Jesus loves me.

I had to ask God to change my heart. I was the person who thought everyone isn't capable of being a friend and that no one was capable of having a real friendship with me. I put a wall up and shut everyone out. I probably missed a whole lot of opportunities when people were trying to show me a real friendship. My mom would always tell me about how not everyone belongs in your inner circle; some people belong in your outer circle. All my life, I have based my "friends" off this principle, and most of those people were automatically placed in the outer circle.

Growing up, my mom used to listen to gospel duo Mary Mary a lot. There was one song that always stuck out to me—"God in Me"—because she would always reference it when she told me that people would be attracted to me because of the God that is in me. It's the God within me that has the ability to be a friend to those who need one, no matter how lonely I get or how irritated others make me. It is as though God is placing them in my life for a reason, or maybe the other way around.

To this day, I still struggle with not having a lot of friends; it's one of my biggest insecurities. I am learning to let people be friends to me and to let go of the belief that people need me more than I need them. Honestly, they don't need me—they really need Jesus. I still pray that God will send me friends that are literally just for me. Someone that I can really call a true friend. Someone who acts like me, relates to me, understands me, and is literally just like me. Someone who helps me achieve my goals and vice versa. Someone who can help and support me as I grow spiritually and for whom I can do the same. More importantly, I am extremely glad that God brought me my best friend, the Holy Spirit. As I read a book titled Your Knight in Shining Armor by P.B. Wilson, it spoke about how Jesus sent His Spirit to comfort us and give us everlasting peace and joy. "The amazing grace of the Master, Jesus Christ, the extravagant love of God, the intimate friendship of the Holy Spirit, be with you all" (2 Cor. 13:14). There is absolutely no better friend to have than the Holy Spirit.

Depression

IN MY GENERATION, IT'S SAD HOW DEPRESSION HAS BECOME SO COMMON. Being stuck in depression has become a norm to society, when it shouldn't be. Honestly, depression is a topic I could talk about for a while. I have been in and out of depression since I was eight. Can you imagine being in the third grade and having depression? I don't even think I knew what depression was in third grade, but I remember the feeling and not being able to shake it.

I doubt that I am the only person who experienced depression at a young age. I believe it started when I was molested by a family member. I can't even begin to tell you what it feels like or how to deal with the emotions that come with it. Thinking back to when it happened to me, I just remember the feelings of weakness, embarrassment, guilt, and complete disbelief. I remember how bad it felt when my own family didn't believe me. After that, my depression just sprang up. I even experienced a lot of depression when it came to my siblings. To make an extremely long story short, my siblings were my enemies—they all hated me. I was the annoying, bratty little sister and the black sheep of my family. Everyone loved my older brother and I felt so lonely and unimportant. I began to resent them and hated going around them. Family gatherings were absolutely horrible for me. I only have three cousins that are my age, and I wasn't really close to any of them. The way they treated me compared to my brother made me feel that my whole family hated me.

From there, everything just escalated. I began to hate everything: my siblings, my parents, my school, my church, even myself. It wasn't until this year that I was told that when I hate myself, I am basically telling Jesus His death on the cross wasn't enough. That convicted my heart more than anything ever had. I couldn't imagine telling Jesus that He wasn't enough for me or that me hating myself was bigger than Him.

People would normally tell me to "snap out" of my depression, but no one knows what that actually means. How do you just "snap out" of depression? The enemy held me in depression for the longest time, really making me believe everything he was telling me. I had never experienced suicidal thoughts like I had during this period in my life. I also never spoke up about my suicidal thoughts to anyone; I didn't want them to think I was being crazy or overdramatic. I thought it was impossible to overcome depression, but I also believe it's up to you—it is a choice that you have to make for yourself. I was always taught not to claim things as though they were my own.

My counselor diagnosed me with severe depression, and my mom instantly told me not to claim it, because that is a stronghold. I believe I got so used to the feeling of pain that when I was in depression, I didn't care whether or not I got out of it.

It was almost as if I was numb to depression. It took many months for me to start speaking life over myself and declaring that the depression would go away. The power of life and death is in your tongue, and your words carry weight. I am by no means perfect, but I do practice what I say and it has helped and still does help me. Prayer actually works, and I fight every day to keep my sanity, because we are in a spiritual warfare and I one-thousand-percent believe that I cannot make it by myself.

Anxiety

JUST LIKE DEPRESSION, I THOUGHT ANXIETY WAS SOMETHING THAT I would never have to go through. I wish I had a time machine so I could go back and warn myself that that's not what happens.

I never experienced anxiety until I experienced depression. To me, they both come as a package deal—like you can't get one without the other. Once experiencing anxiety, I couldn't shake it.

At a young age, I didn't know what anxiety meant, but now that I know, I was anxious about almost everything. I was scared of the future, going to school, going to church, and being alone, and the list goes on forever. Most of all, I fear the unknown. Not knowing makes me feel so uncomfortable, and I dread being blindsided.

I eventually even experienced a huge fear of the demonic. In the summer of 2019, I watched God deliver some of the people dearest to me. After that, I became really afraid of anything that had to do with the demonic, because demons are not respecters of person. They go after innocent children and mess with their minds, so why wouldn't it happen to me?

This was a fear that I had for about two years, and it was hard for me to let go of it.

It was like everywhere I went, the thoughts haunted me. Even talking about the demonic brought so much anxiety. It wasn't until years later, when my aunt and my mom sat me down and told me that whatever happened to them wouldn't happen to me because I have Jesus in me, leaving no room for anything demonic, then I was able to calm down.

Jesus and the enemy cannot live inside you at the same time. I realized I couldn't be fearful because God had not given me the spirit of fear, but the spirit of power, love, and a sound mind (2 Tim. 1:7).

I used to let my anxiety control my whole life. I missed out on amazing opportunities; I missed out on being a kid, as well as doing things that teenagers do because of my anxiety. I had to surrender my anxiety to God because fear is a sin.

You're supposed to fear God and that's it. In the Bible, it says, "Do not be anxious about anything, but in everything, by prayer and petition, with thanksgiving, present your requests to God. And the peace of God, which transcends all understanding, will guard your hearts and your minds in Christ Jesus" (Phil. 4:6-7).

When I was little, I used to sing this song about how God has the whole world in His hands. God literally keeps me in the palm of His hands every day. I choose daily to put my faith in God, and with faith in Him, I have nothing to be anxious about. God didn't give me the spirit of fear but of power, love, and a sound mind.

Insecurities

BEING INSECURE REALLY AND TRULY SUCKS. I CAN'T BEGIN TO DESCRIBE what it's like having to wake up in the same skin, same body shape, same hair, same everything and absolutely hate how you look. I have been insecure pretty much all my life.

Ever since then, those words were attached to me, and I started to believe them.

I began to hate myself and everything and everyone around me. The enemy would replay the words in my head every day. My absolute biggest insecurity has always been my hair. When I first started school, I was the only black child, and I had the typical ponytails with barrettes in my hair. I absolutely hated it. I would always wish to have lighter skin or to not have "black people hair." No one ever taught me how to embrace my hair; therefore, I didn't. On a daily basis, I would get called black, fat, ugly, annoying, and I would get told no one liked me. Every day, I went to school and got teased about how I looked, then I would go home and get teased even more by my siblings.

In middle school, believe it or not, I was a huge bully. To make myself feel better, I would put my insecurities onto other people. In the moment, it made me look cool, but now that I look back at it, I looked a complete mess. I can't believe my friends actually wanted to hang around someone like that.

Since I was super insecure about my hair, I begged my mom to let me straighten my hair, and she did. I thought that I was the next Tyra Banks. No one could tell me anything. Then I got bullied because I had no eyebrows. So, I begged my mom to let me start wearing makeup, and she did, and then I got bullied because I didn't know how to do my eyebrows. I would literally come home crying to my mom every day.

Nothing I did satisfied anybody. No matter what I did, I always managed to get made fun of.

My mom and my family would always tell me that I was beautiful, but I always thought they had to say that because they were supposed to make me feel better. As if middle school wasn't hard enough, high school was a whole other ball park. I would compare myself to everyone. To make it even better, my friends were pretty. So, I wasn't just ugly—I was ugly with super pretty friends.

In high school, I became more insecure than I had ever been. I wasn't a hundred pounds, I didn't have long, pretty hair, I didn't have all the boys chasing after me; I just felt ugly, like a complete disgrace to my family's genes. I had my good days, when I felt like I looked decent enough, but those were very rare.

One thing that used to make me mad was when pretty people would call themselves ugly or say that they hated their hair or how they looked. I used to think, honestly, if only they knew the things that I had to go through, all the tears I shed. Then I talked to one of my close friends, and she told me about her own insecurities. It took me by surprise because in my eyes, she was literally perfect, but she was going through the exact same things I was. This opened my eyes to the fact that we were actually the same—we struggled the same, we hurt the same, we were identical.

I had this weird theory that I was destined to be single forever. That no guy would ever want someone as ugly as me. I believed this until a pastor gave me a prophetic word about how I was going to have kids and God was taking me on a journey where I would meet my husband. I remember going home and sobbing my eyes out, asking God who could possibly love someone who looks like this.

A year went by, and I remember coming into my room, sitting on my bed, and sobbing my eyes out. My mom was the one that came in and found me, and she asked me what was going on. That's when I began to tell her about all of my insecurities and how ugly I felt, and how it really had taken a toll on my life. She knew I was insecure, but she had never known the severity of it. She called my grandpa and started to pray for me, but it wasn't just any kind of prayer—it was a prayer in which you could tell they were really expecting God to do something for me. After they finished praying, I felt indescribable. Words can't express how much peace I felt. My insecurities went away, not completely, but with time, I began to feel more confident in myself and in my skin. It was a daily struggle, but I had to trust in God and believe in what He had created. I had to believe that I was beautiful.

I believe that God created everyone to be beautiful and unique and special in His image. My grandpa always says, "God doesn't make ugly children." I literally have to repeat that to myself and tell myself a thousand times how beautiful I am. With a full face of makeup on or not, I know that God says I am beautiful. Honestly, that's the only opinion that matters to me.

I pray that my story will be able to inspire many girls and boys around the world.

Once you start to accept yourself and be confident in the way you look, you will be able to accomplish a lot. The Bible tells us that God looks at the heart. What's most important is that you look into your heart, and if there's anything that is not of God, ask Him to remove it.

Maturity

BEING MATURE AT MY AGE IS SOMETHING I ACTUALLY FIND KIND OF COOL. I'm the teenager that doesn't get into trouble, get caught in stupidity, get lost in the crazy world of drama, or worry about the tea that's happening, which is only by the grace of God. God has kept me and saved me from making very dumb and unwise decisions. But don't mistake that for my having it all together, because I am not perfect; I have made plenty of dumb decisions, and I also make plenty of mistakes.

At my age, being mature can sometimes be hard, only because most people mistake maturity for being a "know it all," which is false. I honestly don't know everything.

It can also be hard because everyone comes up to you with their problems expecting you to help them or to solve them. Most of the time you don't really have an answer or you don't know what to say. I usually just go off of what the Bible says or what God is telling me. Maturity can make you expect others to act the way you do, but not everyone can act just like you. It almost makes you feel alone sometimes. Then again, you have to realize that you're an original; you're one of a kind. It just depends on your perspective. For me, maturity was a choice; I chose to live the way God created me and left my former mindset behind.

I have received many prophetic words about how God is calling me to be a leader and how I am going to lead my generation to Christ. I can't do that if I am caught up in the world. I have to remind myself daily of the word God has spoken over my life and not allow myself to get distracted from it. I am on a mission to do what God has called me to do, and I am going to achieve it. I just have to keep the right mindset.

Purpose

ALL MY LIFE, I HAVE STRUGGLED TO KNOW WHAT MY PURPOSE WAS. When I went through my phase of depression, I started to believe that there was really no purpose for me in this world. The enemy tried to fight me with my suicidal thoughts and make me feel like I never had a purpose.

Ever since I was a young girl, God has always given me the gift of writing. I wrote songs, kept a journal, and did a lot of other things that I couldn't really quite put a title to, but that I knew were important nonetheless. I mostly wrote songs. I wrote my own stuff and I never really liked it, but I couldn't judge God's taste in music. I never really knew why He gave this gift to me. I realized writing is my passion, but I also have a strong passion for music as well. I could write all day and still have the energy to write more. Eventually, I want to be a songwriter and an author. I became so unsure of what God wanted me to do in this world, until I realized that I am supposed to write—which is strange, because I have hated writing all my life, especially in school. English was never my strong subject.

Recently, God appeared to me in a dream, and I felt peace, confident that I was supposed to write. I knew I had to write this book to help other people my age get through some of the stuff that I have been through. It is sometimes hard to go through things and feel like you're alone. It is reassuring when you realize there are other people with experiences like yours. I believe that my purpose is to share my story to help others just like me and to lead people to Christ as His disciple.

Perseverance

PERSEVERANCE WAS ALWAYS A STRUGGLE FOR ME. I'M THE TYPE OF person to quit when I feel like things are getting hard. My mom always taught me that I don't quit when life gets hard, and my dad always told me to never quit. Persevering is probably one of the hardest things ever. Trying to push when you have nothing left in you is draining and frustrating. It almost makes no sense. God only gives you what you can handle—no more. I always wondered if God thought I was Superman or something, because sometimes I just wanted to call it quits. But now that I look back at it, I thank God for giving me the strength to persevere.

One of my uncles preached a sermon on how we should keep pushing even when we can't feel God. Personally, I would get a prophetic word and be so on fire for God, but then when I couldn't feel His love, I would distance myself from Him because I didn't think He was listening to me.

Then I realized God is the only one who could've helped me through the tough times. I knew that I was not strong enough to do it alone. I recently started a new journey with God, and it became frustrating when I couldn't hear Him or when I felt as if He wasn't there. I knew God was there; He had revealed Himself to me multiple times, and I refused to give up this time. I kept pushing. Now He and I are forming a closer relationship, and it's most definitely the best thing to ever happen to me.

Thankfulness

HAVE YOU EVER MET SOMEONE THAT ALWAYS PICKS THE BAD OUT OF EVERY situation? That is a huge pet peeve of mine. There are so many good things one could focus on, but some people just choose to focus on the bad. Are you breathing? Are you alive? You serve the one and only amazing God—another incredible thing to be thankful for.

I used to be that person who couldn't find any good in life. I was stuck in a dark hole in which it seemed there was nothing good in my life. Then I had a conversation with my mom and my grandpa, and they told me how I should be thankful for everything that I have. Even the little things, because just as fast as God blessed you, He can take it away. That conversation was probably one of the biggest eye-openers I ever had. I had to look at myself, realize how much of a brat I was, and apologize to God for never thanking Him for the little things in life. It's the little things that count, and God blessed me with a billion little things. But somehow, I managed to let the little things slip over my head. I asked God to deal with me and open my eyes to see all the blessings that I had in my life, and how fortunate I was (and am). Once He did that, I haven't been able to be ungrateful since.

Wisdom

WISDOM IS SOMETHING THAT I WISH I WOULD'VE HAD IN MY EARLIER days of childhood.

Wisdom would have helped me to handle certain situations better, and I would have been able to stop so many things if I had been wise. Now God is giving me the gift of wisdom.

Wisdom is where I get my maturity and common sense from. Just like maturity, wisdom is also a very lonely trait. I believe everyone has wisdom—it's just a matter of using it. God blessed me with the wisdom to know right from wrong. I also had a lot of people in my life who helped me and shared a lot of wisdom with me. My church family, for example, has been very influential to me since I was two. I grew up with all the pastors being my aunts and uncles, with Grandpa as the bishop, and they all have been super influential, not only in my spiritual walk with God, but also in my life in general. Additionally, much of my wisdom comes from my mom. She has to be one of the smartest people I know, and she has taught me more than I can remember.

Love

THE DEFINITION OF LOVE IS A DEEP AFFECTION FOR SOMETHING OR someone. I have always thought agape love, which is unconditional love, was the greatest love. We are called to love everyone unconditionally, with no limits, and to know that if no one else loves us, God always does. I struggled with believing that for a while, because I'm such an imperfect being. I mess up numerous times a day, and I just couldn't believe that anyone could ever love someone as horrible as me. Which is crazy to think! All you have to do is ask for forgiveness and God gives it to you. He throws all your sins in the sea of forgetfulness and never brings them back up to throw in your face. It's actually amazing.

After agape love, the next level of love is eros, which is romantic love. Two words: heck no. I promised myself that I'd never fall in love, that I would be single for life; I would live my dream, and my only baby would be my career.

But then I got into middle school, and all of a sudden, I would walk into a room and see where the boys were. I hated it. I became boy crazy and I didn't even notice it.

I had to pray about this, but every time I talked to someone about it, they said it was normal, that it was just my hormones. Even though it was normal, I personally didn't like it.

The next level after eros is philia, as in affectionate. And if you know me, you know I hate any skin-to-skin contact—it's like my biggest pet peeve. My mom's always trying to be more affectionate with me so that I can get over this, but I refuse and I don't know why. However, I am slowly but surely learning to become a more affectionate person, and to allow people to love me.

Lastly, I'm trying to learn self-love. In my head, I make myself smaller than other people. God recently dealt with me about this so much. He asked me why I shrink myself. It completely shocked me. Ever since then, I have tried to love myself and see myself the way God sees me, and I improve every day. Growing up in the church, loving people was a big focus. My grandpa and all my aunts were really big on love because God has called us to love everyone. If there is one thing that I could ever say that they taught me, it would be how to love. Not just with their words but with their actions. There was never a time when anyone came to Restoration and said they didn't feel loved; it's impossible. Every day, I pray that God gives me a heart for His people, and that I will be able to love with no conditions, just like Jesus loves us.

Compassion

COMPASSION IS THE FEELING AND SHOWING OF SYMPATHY AND CONCERN for others. I have always been a compassionate person—even overly compassionate at times. I used to hate that about myself, because people often take advantage of me for it. I can't change it, though, because that's the way I am.

God spoke a word over my life, saying that I have a heart of compassion, and it's almost impossible for me to not be compassionate toward people. It took me a while to embrace this. Now that I have, I love it. Being compassionate shows people you care. Since many of the people that I hang around with and some of my acquaintances face a lot of loneliness, they look for people who care. That's why God sent them to me. My compassion draws people to God. I can never take credit for what God does.

> "Be kind and compassionate to one another, forgiving each other, just as Christ God forgave you." (Ephesians 4:32)

We are all called to be compassionate toward our brothers and sisters and forgive as God has forgiven us.

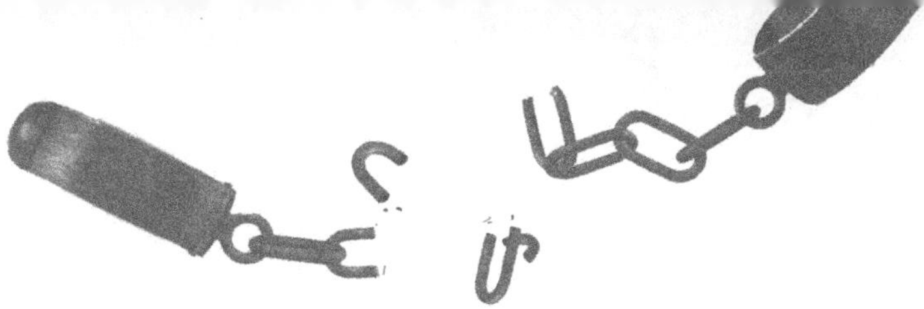

Happiness

IT TAKES A LOT TO MAKE ME TRULY HAPPY. HONESTLY, I CAN ONLY remember a couple times when I was actually truly happy. During most of them, I was probably in the presence of the Lord. There have been times when I was truly happy and didn't even realize it, and there have been times when all I wanted to feel was truly happy, but that happiness seemed so far away.

Happiness is more than just putting a smile on someone's face. To me, happiness is a state of mind I don't want to leave, where I feel joy and I want to stay forever.

It may sound corny, but I truly can say that I find my happiness in Jesus. There's something about knowing that you have a Creator who cares for and loves you no matter what. All you have to do is serve Him and obey Him and He will give you true happiness. Psalm 30:5 says, "For His anger is but for a moment, His favor is for life; weeping may endure for a night, but joy comes in the morning." This scripture is so significant because it shows that we do have rough times, slip up, and get angry, but God will always bring us joy.

Rejoice in knowing you belong to God and allow the Lord into your heart. You will receive true happiness.

About the Author

MY NAME IS LANIAH GOODMAN. I WAS BORN IN MORENO VALLEY, California, and raised in California's Central Valley since the age of two. I am a member of Restoration Ministries. At the age of five, I made the decision to get baptized. From that day until the current, my life has never been the same. I knew that when I came out of the water, when baptized, I was a new person. Bishop Robert Hooks is my bishop and my grandpa. I grew up in church, but going to church does not mean you have a relationship with the Lord. At a young age, I made the decision to have a relationship with Jesus and get to know Him as my personal Lord and Savior.

My parents separated and filed for a divorce 2017, during my freshman year of high school, and I separated myself from God, even though I still attended church. I still prayed, but I was battling depression and anxiety as a result of the divorce and my father's infidelity. In April of 2019, at the end of my sophomore year, I received a prophetic word—this means God used someone to speak a Since that day, my life has never been the same.

Having a relationship with Jesus became a priority for me. Even though I have a relationship with God, I still am human and go through life struggles. I enjoy sleeping and watching YouTube, and TikTok.

My favorite color is blue. I continue to make my quiet time with Jesus is a priority. This means I pray, read my bible, journal every night, and do bible study with my peers over FaceTime. I am also actively involved in our church youth group and serve as a greeter and at times an usher.

I enjoy being surrounded by family, especially my aunts, uncles, cousins, and grandparents. I have two brothers; one is older than I am and the other is younger.

I am my mother's only daughter, as well as the middle child. I have five god-sisters and two god-brothers. I desire to know more about my family history, especially those that have passed away. I have plenty of family on my father's side that I do not know but I would like to get to know. My father and his family are from Central California and my mother was born and raised in Southern California. I am a super big mommy's girl.

My mom is my best friend, my mentor, and my spiritual counselor; she's the best person on the planet! I am a huge family person, which is strange because I wasn't always like that. I love going to Southern California and spending time with my family, which, unfortunately, doesn't happen often. I am a person of many pet peeves; I hate being touched and being barefoot. I don't like people who are dishonest. There's a lot more but it would take forever for me to explain.

Overall, I am a super sweet and relaxed person. I love seeing people happy, and I love joking around and making people laugh. I am a giver, like my mom. This means I don't mind giving the shirt off my back to someone in need or helping others, period. I love talking to my god-sisters on the phone and spending time with them.

Academically, I am a senior in high school and a straight-A student. I have been involved in leadership at my high school since my sophomore year. As a sophomore, I was president of one of the clubs on campus for two years in a row, served over two years in ASB, three years in Avid, and served as youth leader at my church. I have been asked to join multiple panel discussions with Visalia Unified School district representing the voice of our students and those of my culture. I am the one person everyone comes to for advice and to tell their problems to. I consider it a privilege that God would use me to pray for and guide my peers in the right direction. My ultimate desire is for them to know Jesus like I do.

It's funny, but I am pretty shy until I get to know you. In the second month of my senior year, I was accepted into the first college of my choice, Fresno Pacific University. I also received a grant of $24,000 from the dean. I am currently attending bible college at Golden Grain. My life is busy between youth groups at church, attending church, being active in leadership at school, and being a mentor to my peers. I can truly say that I am a blessed woman of God. In the year 2020, I purchased my first car, wrote this book and a children's book, and am currently working on a third book. God gives me what to write and I do it. I take no credit from anything I've been through or accomplished.

God has been with me along the way. I enjoy writing and I hope this book blesses you and you understand that you are never alone because Jesus is with you. He is only waiting for you to ask Him for help.

As you read this book, you have become familiar with my struggles in life over the years, and if God brought me through such horrific times in my life, He can do the same for you!

CPSIA information can be obtained
at www.ICGtesting.com
Printed in the USA
LVHW091655010921
696699LV00001B/2

9 781662 815058